CW00430818

The Art of Marriage

Wilferd Arlan Peterson

Illustrated by Chris Molan

SOUVENIR PRESS

Happiness in marriage is not something that just happens. A good marriage must be created. In the art of marriage the *little things* are the *big things* . . .

It is never being too old
to hold hands.

It is remembering to say, "I love you," at least once each day.

It is never going to sleep angry.

It is at no time taking the other for granted; the courtship shouldn't end with the honeymoon, it should continue through all the years.

It is having a mutual sense of values
and common objectives;
it is standing together
facing the world.

It is forming a circle of love
that gathers in the whole family.

It is doing things for each other, not
in the attitude of duty or sacrifice,
but in the spirit of joy.

It is speaking words of appreciation
and demonstrating gratitude
in thoughtful ways.

It is not expecting the husband to wear a halo or the wife to have the wings of an angel. It is not looking for perfection in each other.
It is cultivating flexibility, patience, understanding and a sense of humour.

It is having the capacity to forgive and forget.

It is giving each other an atmosphere
in which each can grow.

It is finding room for the things of the spirit. It is a common search for the good and the beautiful.

It is not only marrying the right partner, it is *being* the right partner.

'Wherever she was,
there was Eden."

Mark Twain